Anger

Escaping the Maze

Resources for Changing Lives

A Ministry of
THE CHRISTIAN COUNSELING AND
EDUCATIONAL FOUNDATION
Glenside, Pennsylvania

RCL Ministry Booklets
Susan Lutz, Series Editor

Anger

Escaping the Maze

David Powlison

P U B L I S H I N G
P.O. BOX 817 • PHILLIPSBURG • NEW JERSEY 08865-0817

What is anger? How should we handle it? In a world of disappointments, imperfections, miseries, and sins (our own and others'), anger is a given. You get angry. I get angry. No wonder the Bible comes packed with stories, teachings, and comments about anger. God intends us to understand anger and to know how problems of anger can be resolved.

According to the Bible, even God gets angry—at sin and evil. The fact that he does tells us that anger can be utterly right, good, appropriate, beautiful, the only fair response to something evil, and the loving response on behalf of evil's victims. But Satan is angry as well. Anger like his is utterly wrong, bad, inappropriate, ugly—a completely destructive response. Such anger summons the very essence of evil: "I want my way and not God's, and because I can't have my way, I rage."

Anger is natural to human beings in two very different ways. It is natural because we were created in God's image with the capacity for godly anger. But sinful anger is also natural to us since the Fall. As human beings corrupted into the image of Satan, we are also hard-wired for resentment and hatred. And in a fallen world, human anger is so disordered that even righteously aroused anger easily degenerates into something sinful.

This brings us back to our opening questions: What is anger and how should we handle it? Our world offers answers that are governed by many harmful misconceptions and outright lies. But the Bible's answers offer hope and power to people trapped in their struggles with anger. Its truth provides a pathway out of anger and the maze of lies and confusion that surrounds it.

If you feel helpless to overcome anger, be encouraged! God does not show us our sins to leave us trapped in them. Jesus came to defeat anger's power in your life, and his wisdom can guide you as you do battle against it. Let's begin by looking at three of the most common and harmful misconceptions about anger that plague our society and our personal lives.

Lie #1: Anger Is Something Inside Me

The Bible makes it clear that anger is not a "thing." It is a moral act of the whole person, not a "substance" or a "something" inside you. That might sound obvious, but most popular understandings of anger don't see it. Is anger a hot, emotional fluid that builds up pressure inside? Or is anger a demon that takes up residency? These common ideas—opposed to each other in every other way!—both agree that anger is a *something*.

In Western culture, many theories of anger treat it as an emotional fluid that builds up pressure inside and must be released. This "hydraulic" theory of anger contributes to the pop wisdom that anger "just is, and is neither good nor bad." Why does this theory seem plausible? Because images such as the following capture what anger can feel like: A person's anger can be "pent up"; "his pump is primed." People can be "boiling mad," "filled" with anger, waiting to "explode." They "blow off steam." Old, unresolved anger can be "stored up inside," "harbored" for decades. If you "get it off your chest" so that your anger is "spent," you feel better. All these metaphors depict anger as a pressurized substance inside us.

No doubt, these colorful descriptions *do* capture how anger feels. But a metaphor is not meant to overpower the thing it intends to illustrate. Anger feels fiery, but it's not a fire. The solution to sinful anger is not to surgically remove the furnace or to drink enough water to quench the flames! The solution is a moral one: to "turn" from sin to God's grace in repentant faith.

When people believe that anger is something inside them, not something they do, it points them to a solution other than repentance. Counseling will seek to release pressure by "lancing the boil" (another metaphor!). "Here's a pillow. Call it your mom. Take this baseball bat and wallop the pillow, cursing her out for everything she did. You'll get the anger out of your system, and you'll be fixed."

The scenario sounds logical only if anger is a *thing* inside us. But because anger is a moral act of the whole person, the scenario is sinful, even if it does take the edge off the anger temporarily. The true solution is self-understanding, an acknowledgment of wrong, repentance, faith, and new obedience by the power of God's grace.

In animistic cultures—and in some segments of contemporary Christian culture—many people treat anger as a "demon." Again, anger is *something* inside you, and you will be fixed by getting it out of you, in this case by casting it out. Again, the theory seems plausible. Anger, as much as any sin, makes us exactly like the Devil. When you see (or are) a sinfully angry person, the Devil's image is displayed.

But the Devil's hand in anger is no different from his involvement in any other sin. He does not demonize us into sin; he rules us. He tempts and lies in order to control and destroy us. The solution lies not in exorcism from supposed demons of rage, anger, pride, and rebellion; it lies in *repentance* from rage, anger, pride, and rebellion, turning to the Lord of grace.[1] Anger is a moral act, and its solution is a moral act, too.

Lie #2: It's Okay to Be Angry at God

Anger at God is commonplace. The Bible speaks of it scores of times.[2] It's one of the most logical human reactions, given the nature of sin, but it's a deadly wickedness. What Job's wife said was terrible advice, but at least she had her facts straight: "Curse God and die!" (Job 2:9).

Many popular psychologies discuss anger at God in a very unhelpful way. The standard therapeutic formula says something like this: "If you are angry at God, you need to do four things. First, remember anger just is, it's neither good nor bad. It's okay to feel angry at God. He made us with angry emotions. Second, God often lets us down and disappoints us. How else can we explain being abused and crying out to him for deliverance, yet the abuse continued? If he's supposed to be in control, then he could have stopped it, and he didn't. Third, you need to ventilate your anger at God. He can absorb your honest anger. So don't be afraid to tell him exactly what you feel and think. Many psalms portray anger at God, so if other godly people have let out their rage at him, you can too. Say it like you feel it so you won't be a hypocrite. Fourth, you need to forgive God. You need to let go of the hostility to be at peace with yourself and to build a trusting relationship with God. Forgive him for the ways he let you down."

Plausible? To some. Coherent? It does hang together. True? No way.

Anger at God is profitably examined by asking, "What do you want and believe?"—just as you would with any other instance of anger. What you will invariably find is that your heart is controlled by desires and lies that have been substituted for the living and true God. For example, if I crave marriage and believe that God will reward my devotion to him with a wife, my heart sets itself up for anger at God if that desire is not satisfied.

The anger at God that is frequently seen in counseling is almost always (we'll discuss those "anger" psalms in a moment) sinful anger. It overflows with malice and mistrust toward God. It firmly embraces (and proclaims) lies about what he is like. It rationalizes self-destructive and sinful behaviors. But anger at God, handled rightly, presents a wonderful opportunity to understand your own heart. By the grace of God, those who are angry with him can often discover for the first time who he actually is, and who they are as well.

Let's examine psychology's therapeutic formula point by point.

First, we've seen that anger is not neutral. Anger toward God will either maliciously accuse him or express living faith in him. Our angry emotions may be either godly or devilish. In contrast, the first piece of therapeutic advice entirely avoids this moral dilemma.

Second, does God let us down when we suffer? Nowhere in the Bible do we find a shred of evidence that God ever truly betrays us. The Bible discusses suffering constantly, but it always shows us that any apparent "betrayal" by God must be seen in the context of his larger purposes. Certainly, people may truly and seriously let us down. Abusers betray trust in such a heinous way that they deserve hell's deepest pit.[3] Certainly the Devil torments us. That's what he's about. Certainly suffering hurts. Anger toward tyrants and the arch-tyrant is certainly justified. And groaning (to God, in faith and hope) about our sufferings is right and good too.

But God has never promised freedom from tears, mourning, crying, and pain—or from the evils that cause them—until the great day when life and joy triumph forever over death and misery. The interweaving of God's glory and our well-being is far bigger than people imagine. People who are angry with God have often believed false promises or overlaid their own (unjustified) expectations upon God. They have then become angry with a "disappointing" God, sometimes even confusing his actions and motives with Satan's and with evil people who imitate the Devil's cruelty.

It is curious how people who don't *really* believe in the sovereignty of God act as if they do ("He could have changed things and didn't") when they are angry at him. To *really* believe in God's sovereignty is to gain an unshakable foundation for trust in the midst of even hellish torments, let alone the milder pains.

The real God is the *deliverer* from tyrants. He is the only hope of the "poor, afflicted, needy, unfortunate, and oppressed." And—a truth so profound that we can only say it with trembling—when we are honest with ourselves, we realize that the line between good and evil runs through *every* heart except God's. We are more like the tyrants than unlike them. It's not that we deserved what others did to us. That was simply evil, and it will be dealt with fully and justly by God. But that does not mean that we are thereby innocent people. We also deserve wrath for our *own* sins. And here, Jesus suffered the tortures we fairly deserve.

The anger at God that counselors often see typically masks self-righteousness and expresses blatant unbelief. But the world's therapeutic formula never challenges that. Because it never talks about the sinfulness within anger at God, the therapeutic formula can never offer the only true hope for such strugglers: the Savior who will deliver his people from the condemnation and corruption of their own sins, and from the pain of other people's sins.

The Bible challenges the third point in the therapeutic formula, too. You do not need to ventilate your sinful anger at God in order to deal with it. You need to repent of it, like Job. You need to understand the demands, the false beliefs, the self-righteousness that produce and drive it.

There is no psalm that encourages the venting of hostile anger. In the "anger" psalms, without exception, what breathes through is an attitude of faith. Yes, there is true upset, complaint, hurt, and dismay. We can reverently call it righteous anger because it yearns for God's glory and the well-being of his people. It yearns to have God eliminate the sufferings we currently experience. The intensity of the complaint arises from the intensity of the faith. But it contains no cursing, no bitterness, no lies, no scorn or hostile belittling, no blasphemies.

The psalmists are dismayed because they know and trust that God is good, because they love him, and because they struggle to reconcile his promises with their present struggle. The psalmists move *toward* God in honest faith, wrestling with their circumstances. But people angry at God shove him away. The psalmists want God's glory and want evil to go away; they groan and complain *in their faith*. And typically, they have an awareness of guilt and sin; they recognize that suffering in general is somehow deserved, even though they may hate the evil intents of those who bring it.

When the Bible teaches us how to express our pain to God, it teaches a cry of faith, not a roar of blasphemous rage. The therapeutic alternative is too distorted to teach troubled people how and why to complain to a God they love.

Fourth, the notion of forgiving God is a final blasphemy in a string of blasphemies. We as sinners have no right to "forgive" God, and God has no need of it. This twisted attempt at reconciliation stands in sharp contrast to the path taken by the person who deals with anger at God by repentance and faith. This person is no longer angry because his anger has been replaced by an overwhelming gratitude. This is because he has *found* forgiveness, not because he has *granted* it. God is *good*. He does not need our forgiveness! He never stands in the dock as the accused, no matter how much our sinful anger seeks to put him there.

Even Job, a godly man of honest faith, repented at the end for his strand of self-righteousness. To the degree that he had blamed God and sought to justify himself, he was brought to admit that he was wrong. That is what the book of Job is about.

Every step in the world's therapeutic formula is bent to one end: keeping man on the throne of pride. The person who is honest about his or her anger at God—and gets to the truth about it—will walk a very different path. The repentant and believing heart will not settle for an uneasy truce between past sufferings and an unreliable deity. The believing heart will find truth, joy, hope, and love unspeakable. The believing heart will find God.

Lie #3: My Big Problem Is Anger at Myself

Many of the problems we've just discussed reappear in current ideas on self-forgiveness. If I'm angry at myself—and the phenomenon is a common one—current wisdom argues that I chiefly need to forgive myself. Among Christians, two reasons are usually given. First, "God did not create junk, and since he created me I must be worth something." Second, "Jesus thought I was so valuable that he loved me and came to die for me." Therefore, I can feel good about myself, and view my failings more tolerantly. End result? I "forgive myself" instead of being angry with myself.[4] This sounds reasonable to many people. But it's misguided.

Why are people angry at themselves? First, invariably they have failed to live up to some standard. That standard may be bogus—needing a house that looks like the pages of *House Beautiful*; getting straight A's; being able to please an unpleasable parent; having a textbook quiet time. Or the standard may be accurate—not committing adultery, not having an abortion, not being lazy. In either case, there is something I believe I should live up to. But I fail.

Second, anger always requires a judge, because they are the ones who make judgments. In the Old Testament metaphor, something can be displeasing "in my eyes" or "in your eyes" or "in the eyes of the Lord." Whose eyes are doing the judging when I am angry with myself? My own. This is why self-haters never get much satisfaction out of well-meaning attempts to help them believe in God's forgiveness in Christ. They may "already believe" that God has forgiven them for the messy house or the abortion, but it isn't enough: "*I* can't forgive *myself*." And to them, their eyes are more significant than God's.

Frequently people who "can't forgive themselves" serve both their own eyes and the eyes of others. I want my house to look impeccable to please myself *and* to impress my mother and neighbors. When my house is messy, I loathe myself. I have failed to please both myself and others.

Or I may have accurate standards (against abortion) but the wrong eyes. In my eyes I "can't forgive myself" for having had an abortion. How could *I* have done that? *I* must make up for it, or *I* must suffer for it. That is highly self-righteous all the way around: I simultaneously play judge, criminal, and savior, and know nothing of the righteousness of Christ that makes the New Testament sing for joy.

Or I may be preoccupied with the judgments of others. I'm ashamed to have anyone know about the abortion. They might think ill of me. The Bible terms this the fear of man, substituting social opinion for the fear of the Lord. The eyes that self-haters live before are often a composite of what the Bible calls pride and the fear of man.

Third, when I set up the standard and the eyes that judge me, I also create my definition of a "savior." To make up for my failure to meet my own (or others') standards, I may strive to attain perfection. I work twice as hard at housecleaning. I compulsively minister in the pro-life movement. But it doesn't work. The house keeps getting messy, and the abortion still blots my past. I decide to keep trying to play my own savior by rebuilding a perfect record, which (if only I could do it) would make everything better. But I fail. So self-hatred always has the last word.

People in this situation need help to rethink all three points: standards, "eyes," and saviors. Their counterfeit reality has left them confused and unhappy, and only truth can bring them wisdom and joy.

If you want to help, first search out whether the standards they use to judge themselves are God's, their own, or ones they have borrowed from others (such as Mom and neighbors). Sometimes the standards will be accurate; many times the standards will be distorted and can be challenged and changed in the light of truth.

Second, whose eyes—whose approval—supremely matter? If I live before my own eyes, I'm substituting my conscience for God. This is an act of pride. To live before other's eyes—for their approval—is to substitute their evaluation for God's. This is an act of man-fearing. To live in God's eyes is the beginning of wisdom. The self-hater who awakens to this awakens to reality. He becomes aware of sins he never suspected and of his real need for forgiveness.

Third, who is the proposed savior from all

this chaos and misery? Does the person look to his own efforts to find perfection? Does he punish himself for the guilt of his perceived failures? Jesus Christ alone can bear guilt and give perfection. He can forgive the genuine transgressions (adultery, abortion, laziness); the trust and faith in false standards (*House Beautiful*); the choice to live before eyes other than God's (my own and Mom's); and the pursuit of a self-attained righteousness as a false savior.

Jesus gives a real righteousness—his own perfect life—to people who sin. He gives real forgiveness—his perfect self-sacrifice to bear our punishment—to people who sin. He gives indwelling power—his Holy Spirit—to renew our minds, give us joy, and change us. Case closed: no longer "angry at myself," yet not a whiff of "I need to forgive myself."

Notice, by the way, how the false analysis led to a false gospel (Angry at yourself? Forgive yourself.), just as it did when we considered anger at God. In the biblical scenario, there is no hint of "You are worth so much because of creation, and Jesus' love shows how valuable you are, so you can feel okay about yourself." The truth is, creation and redemption don't give us much reason to feel good about ourselves in and of ourselves. Our creation was in the image of the God of glory, yet look how far we have fallen: "The hearts of the sons of men are full of evil, and insanity is in their hearts throughout their lives" (Ecclesiastes 9:3 NASB).

Similarly, our redemption was won in a way that displays how utterly bad and helpless we are. The only good and worthy Man freely died for ungodly, weak, sinful enemies. Those facts hardly offer a reason for confident self-acceptance and self-forgiveness! Grace, by definition, ruins self-worth. The covert pride that inhabits "low self-esteem" and "anger at myself" is not cured by mislabeling me as valuable in my own right. The biblical gospel points us to the worth of Jesus Christ, who redeemed the unworthy. How much better is this real gospel, which defines our need for forgiveness from God (not ourselves), and provides it completely and freely. People who embrace God's grace become truly happy, free of the need for props to their wobbly self-concept. An accurate, biblical self-knowledge destroys the supposed need for self-esteem. It produces the only people on the planet with reasons for confidence as they approach life.

A Pathway Out of Anger

Let's move in a positive direction. How can we take the biblical teaching on anger to help us change? All that we've looked at thus far can be summarized in eight very practical questions. The first four questions help assess anger; the second four lead to resolution.[5]

Let me use as an example a simple situation that tempts many of us to get angry. You're in a traffic jam and running late for an important noon appointment. It's five minutes before noon, and you are stuck on the highway ten miles away, in traffic that has not moved for twenty minutes. One common response? You snarl—with anger, frustration, disgust, dismay, unhappiness, tension. When you do, ask yourself these questions.

Questions to Assess Anger

Question #1: What is my situation? Anger is provoked. It happens in situations, in specific times and places with specific people. What is happening to me? I was not tempted to anger until I knew I'd be late for my appointment. The significant situation includes the Department of Transportation that is doing the road work, the traffic, the time, the appointment, the possible reaction of the person waiting for me, and so forth.

Question #2: How do I react? This question is meant to help me identify the specific ways I express sinful anger. What is happening in my thought life? Mentally cursing the transportation department? Playing out anxious scenarios of how to make excuses to the person I'm meeting? Self-recrimination, perhaps: "Why didn't I leave earlier, or take a different route, or listen to the traffic report? What if the person I'm supposed to meet gets disgusted with me?"

Where is God in all this? Perhaps I've cursed, invoking his wrath to serve my frustrations. Perhaps I've even thought angry thoughts about God: "Christianity doesn't work; God's a joke; what's the use?"

What about my body and emotions? I feel angry, irritated. The longer I sit here, the more I feel steam coming out my ears. I'm tense. My stomach is churning. I feel anxiety about missing the meeting.

And my actions? Do I creep up to the bumper ahead and not let anyone merge from the sides? Strike my fist on the dashboard? Vent my disgust: "I can't believe it! This is ridiculous! Of all the . . ."? Flip the radio on and off aggressively? Make an obscene gesture or comment? Drive like a maniac once the traffic clears? Let out a semi-coherent burst of anger and excuses when I finally arrive at the appointment?

This stew of anger (and some fear) is a classic "works of the flesh" human reaction.

Question #3: What are my motives? If I'm grumbling and complaining, some set of cravings and false beliefs must be driving me. I need to ask basic questions: "What do I really want? What do I really believe?" The anger comes out of my heart; it's not caused by the situation.[6] Here are some possible rulers of the heart:

- "I want to get where I want to go when I want to get there." That's plain old pride.
- "What will the people think of me? I was late once before." That's fear of man.
- "I need the money this sales call was sure to produce" (or the cure that doctor was sure to provide; or the love that person was sure to give me; or . . .). These are varied cravings ("I want") and false beliefs ("I need") regarding money, medicine, love.

When these cravings (classic "lusts of the flesh") and false beliefs rule my life, they produce sinful anger. If God ruled my life, I might feel disappointment, but I wouldn't be floundering in the swamp.

Question #4: What are the consequences? Anger has consequences. It creates vicious circles. Perhaps as drivers aggressively edge forward, I grind into the car next to me and get an earful of the driver's hostility and a $250 charge on my insurance deductible. Perhaps I reap emotional and physical consequences: guilt, tension, stomachache, and headache. Sometimes the consequences are fatal: the obscene gesture leads to someone firing a gun. Perhaps when I finally arrive at the appointment, I'm so flustered and full of excuses that I make a terrible impression and lose the sale (or girlfriend).

Questions Leading to Resolution of Anger

The first four questions have dissected the anger reaction. They point out the specific provocation, the detailed stew of reactions, the underlying motives, and the consequences. We've glimpsed the vicious circles that define "sin and misery." The next four questions move toward biblical resolution by the grace of the God who has known what's been going on the whole time.

Question #5: What is true? Who is God? What does he say? Here are three biblical themes and truths that are always important when dealing with anger.

First, God is present and in control of this and every other situation. His sovereignty surrounds the things I face in question #1. I will solve sinful anger as I learn to believe, "God is extremely relevant when I'm stuck in traffic. He is present and he is up to something good in my life as his child. God's overriding purpose is to remake me into the image of Jesus Christ, to make me a person slow to anger and full of trust. I don't like the fact that I've missed my appointment, but God has handed me a perfect opportunity to become a different sort of person."

Second, God's law speaks to events such as this. The law acts as both a mirror and a lamp. First, God holds up a mirror to me: Love the Lord your God with all your heart, soul, mind, and strength; and love your neighbor as yourself (Deut. 6:5; Matt. 22:37, 39). The first of those two great commandment lays bare my heart: What did I love instead? I got annoyed because I loved my way, human approval, and money (or health, or love). This command diagnoses the things I found out about myself in question #3. In fact, it taught me to ask those sorts of questions!

The second great commandment helps me to see what works of the flesh emerged from those cravings. The sinful reactions of question #2 are exposed for what they are. I'm even taught what to look for by the multitude of biblical examples and precepts that flow out of this command.[7]

God also holds out the law as a lamp to guide me. The first great commandment tells me to love (and trust, fear, hope in, turn to)

God. I can trust his provision for me financially (or for health, or friendship/marriage) instead of lusting after these things. I can love him for bringing wisdom's clarity and sense into a situation that had been an emotional swamp. It tells me how to meet and know God (question #6, below).

The second great commandment speaks positively of considering the interests of others. How will that apply in a traffic jam? I could be charitable as the traffic merges, and let someone in. If possible, I could call the person waiting for me to let him know the situation. This command speaks of patience and of numerous other good fruits that apply in different life situations. It reminds me to tell the truth when people ask what happened. It challenges me to gain the wisdom I need to apply God's will into this exact situation—at 11:55 A.M. when stuck in traffic and late for an appointment (question #7, below).

Third, God's truth speaks of Jesus. I have been convicted of violating the first and second great commandments in this small incident on the highway. These are sins. And the gospel is the bridge between the law as mirror and the law as lamp, between the chaos of sin and the joys of wisdom. Jesus Christ forgives sins, restores me to God, provides power to be different, and gives hope bigger than the disappointments of life. God is a very present help in trouble and can give me grace to act peacefully and charitably as I ride out the traffic jam. I can know and rejoice in the gift of the love of God.

Question #6: How can I turn to God for help? *Do it.* Question #5 laid out the world-view in which problems now make sense. Mere analysis, however, won't change me. Question #6 gets me moving. God wants me to seek him, to interact with him. I need to apply the truths of question #5, for example, by distinguishing between righteous and sinful anger. It's not hard to tell that my anger fails the test of righteous anger: this traffic jam is *not* a moral evil! My anger has arisen because I served the false gods identified in question #3.

I need to turn from the desires and deeds of the flesh to the Lord of life. I need to confess my sins, ask forgiveness, believe the gospel, ask for the wisdom to know how to respond and the power to do it. The results of all this will be the clear-mindedness of "coming to my right mind." I will know genuine gratitude to God, and contentment (still in the traffic jam, no less) that was inconceivable while I soaked in my sins. I am experiencing the blessing of wanting wisdom more than my way or impressing people or getting money or the other things that threw me into a tailspin.

Question #7: How should I respond in this situation to glorify God? *Do it.* Repentance and faith lead to concrete changes in behavior, emotion, thoughts. Righteousness is just as specific as the sins described in question #2. At the simplest level, I may simply take a deep breath and relax, trusting that God is indeed in control. But God has other fruits in mind, too. I become a charitable, courteous driver. What does it matter if I'm two more car lengths behind? I'll let a couple of cars in. God has set me free of both the hostile and competitive aspects of sinful anger. The traffic jam is no longer a dog-eat-dog battle. I offer thanks to God. I plan what I will say to the person I've stood up: not anxious excuse-making or blustering irritation, but the simple facts, an apology, and a concern for his welfare.

Instead of that mix of anger, anxiety, confusion, and disgruntlement, I'm peaceful with the grateful peace "which transcends all understanding" and the "secret of being content" that come from living in the light of Christ (Phil 4:7, 12). Question #7 tackles every aspect of the situation described in question #1 and walks out the will of God in detail in my world.

Question #8: What are the consequences of faith and obedience? We've already mentioned some of the subjective benefits. More objectively, maybe a dented fender or even a killing was prevented. Somebody else was kept from stumbling into sinful anger or murder on my account. And in the half dozen cars around me, maybe my courtesy and relaxed response prove catching.

Here we come full circle and find that godliness, while not guaranteed to change the original situation, often has an effect for good on the world. Maybe I end up making the sale anyway because the manager is so impressed at the calm, reasonable way in which I handled a frustrating situation. He'd seen too many other salesmen come in spouting excuses. Godliness intrigued and attracted him.

The possibilities for the many-sided blessings of God are endless. Instead of my day being ruined, God has extricated me from sin and misery, and this is perhaps one of the most significant days in my life from the standpoint of growing into the image of Christ. I've learned how life works in God's world. I've learned how the gospel works. I've learned profound lessons in a very tiny corner of life.

And perhaps when I talk to a troubled, distraught friend that evening on the phone, I'm able to "comfort those in any trouble with the comfort [I myself] have received from God" (2 Cor. 1:4). I didn't suffer much—the inconvenience of a traffic jam—and maybe he or she is suffering a great deal. But the dynamic of the human heart is identical: I will understand my friend's temptations to anger, fear, and despair because I've understood my own. And I've come to understand the way of escape. Walking this through has not only blessed me, but has made me able to wisely counsel others.

A traffic jam—that's only a tiny case study. Some people might ask, "What does this have to do with major afflictions and major provocations to anger?" In the way the Bible views things, it has everything to do with them. The same truths about God apply in the same way. Sure, many details will differ. And the Bible is frank: there are tears that won't be wiped away and enemies who won't be out of the way until the last day.

Question #8 does not create heaven on earth. But it creates tastes of heaven, even though the last enemy has not yet been put under Christ's feet. If on the day I see Christ I will be made completely like him, then in a small way I taste the joy of heaven in a traffic jam by being made a bit more like him. These eight questions orient us to *Christian* reality, which is to say they orient us to reality! They teach us about our world, ourselves, our God, how to live. If God teaches you how to handle traffic jams, he will teach you how to handle anything.

Endnotes

1 See my *Power Encounters: Reclaiming Spiritual Warfare* (Grand Rapids: Baker, 1995) for a more extensive critique.

2 It speaks perhaps most vividly in the sustained hostility toward Jesus Christ and those messengers of God who preceded and followed him (especially David, Jeremiah, John the Baptist, and Paul). In the wilderness, grumbling expressed angry displeasure with God. In Proverbs 19:3 a foolish man "rages" against the Lord. In Revelation 16 it says three times that men "blasphemed God" rather than repent.

3 I'm citing a worst-case scenario. Many people who are angry with God have suffered more mild hardships. I've been struck that people who are angry with God have typically suffered the exact same hardships as people who love God!

4 It is probably truer that the therapeutic goal is actually to "accept myself as basically okay, with understandable shortcomings like everyone else," not to "forgive myself." Forgiveness implies that something is so wrong that "without the shedding of blood there is no forgiveness" (Heb. 9:22). The self-forgiveness teaching inhabits the world of humanistic self-acceptance, not Christian forgiveness.

5 This basic framework applies to other problems besides anger. It is simply a summary of the biblical pattern of change.

6 After all, if I had really wanted to avoid the appointment, I would be delighted at being stuck in traffic

with a great excuse! Sinful happiness is a problem for which people rarely seek counsel.

7 Of course, the Bible does not need to or claim to list every single detail. It teaches us what sinful anger looks like and gives us numerous examples, making us wise to discern other examples. For example, I don't need a proof text to know that the act of "buying *Penthouse* and masturbating as a temper tantrum at God" expresses sinful anger. Such an analysis is implicit in "The deeds of the flesh are evident, [fifteen examples], and things like these" (Gal. 5:19–21 NASB). That passage and others give us enough variations on the theme of anger to enable us to get the picture. Biblical categories cover the details of individual situations sufficiently, perfectly, and wisely.

David Powlison *is a counselor and faculty member at the Christian Counseling and Educational Foundation, Glenside, Pennsylvania, and editor of* The Journal of Biblical Counseling.

RCL Ministry Booklets

A.D.D.: Wandering Minds and Wired Bodies, by Edward T. Welch

Anger: Escaping the Maze, by David Powlison

Depression: The Way Up When You Are Down, by Edward T. Welch

Domestic Abuse: How to Help, by David Powlison, Paul David Tripp, and Edward T. Welch

Forgiveness: "I Just Can't Forgive Myself!" by Robert D. Jones

God's Love: Better than Unconditional, by David Powlison

Homosexuality: Speaking the Truth in Love, by Edward T. Welch

"Just One More": When Desires Don't Take No for an Answer, by Edward T. Welch

Marriage: Whose Dream? by Paul David Tripp

Pornography: Slaying the Dragon, by David Powlison

Pre-Engagement: 5 Questions to Ask Yourselves, by David Powlison and John Yenchko

Priorities: Mastering Time Management, by James C. Petty

Suffering: Eternity Makes a Difference, by Paul David Tripp

Teens and Sex: How Should We Teach Them? by Paul David Tripp

Thankfulness: Even When It Hurts, by Susan Lutz